MAKING MEETINGS WORK
A Practical Guide

Alan Barker

The Industrial Society

First published in 1993 by
The Industrial Society
Robert Hyde House
48 Bryanston Square
London W1H 7LN
Telephone: 0171-262 2401

British Library Cataloguing-in-Publication Data
A catalogue record for this book is available from the
British Library.

Typeset by: Action Typesetting Ltd, Gloucester
Printed by: Optichrome Ltd., Woking, Surrey

Text illustrations: Sophie Grillet

The Industrial Society is a Registered Charity No. 290003

658.456/BRR

For Sheridan
who was always in a meeting

Contents

Preface   x

Chapter One: What is a Meeting?   1

How much do your meetings cost?   1
Why have meetings?   2
Why meetings fail   4
How to make meetings work   6

Chapter Two: Before the Meeting   8

The Chair: setting the agenda   9
  Why are we meeting?   10
  Who is involved?   10
  Where are we meeting?   13
  When is the meeting being held?
    (and when will it end?)   15
  What goes on the agenda?   17
  How will the meeting be run?   20

The Administrator's role   21

Preparation for Participants   23

Chapter Three: During the Meeting 27

How groups work 27

Chairing the meeting 29
  Opening the meeting 30
  Keeping control 32
  Discussing each item 33
  Encouraging contributions 34
  Questions and statements 35
  Summarizing 36
  Closing the meeting 37

The Administrator as minute-taker 38
  Listening 38
  Note-taking 39

Participating well 42

Speaking in meetings 44

Making a presentation 46
  Preparing the presentation 47
  Organizing your material 48
  Opening and closing 49
  Visual aids 51
  Answering questions 52

Non-verbal communication 53
  Eyes 53
  Body language 54

Problem people and how to deal with them 55

Problem situations and how to handle them 58
  Loss of direction 58
  Hijacking 59
  Conflict 59
  Groupthink 60

Chapter Four: After the Meeting   62

The Chair: getting action   63

The Administrator: writing the minutes   65
     Constructing a minute   66
     Paragraphs   67
     Sentence length   68
     Unnecessary dialogue   68
     Passive verbs   69
     Tense   70
     Ambiguous wording   71

Participating after the meeting   72

**Chapter Five: Different Meetings
and How to Run Them**   74

Team meetings   74
Problem solving   77
Brainstorming sessions   79
Consultative meetings   81
Mealtime meetings   83
Electronic meetings   84
Multicultural meetings   85
     Language   88
     Preparation   88
     During the meeting   89
     After the meeting   89

Appendices   91

A: Agendas and minutes   91

B: Auditing meetings   95

Bibliography   99

Preface

Four million hours a day: that is one estimate of the amount of time spent in meetings – in the UK alone! Sometimes it feels like it. This book will give you clear guidelines to help make meetings more efficient and enjoyable. Chapter One asks why meetings are held, why so many fail, and how we can make them work. Chapters Two to Four take us through the meeting process – before, during and after – from three points of view:

- The Chair

- The Administrator

- The Participants

These are the names of the principal players in

meetings and for that reason I have given them capital letters throughout. Ideally, no one person should take on more than one of these roles in any one meeting; in reality, of course, they do sometimes overlap.

Chapter Five looks at different kinds of business meeting and the special considerations that apply to each.

What is a meeting?

Fifty million meetings happen every day. They are one of the most common forms of communication at work.

They are also probably the most expensive.

How Much Do Your Meetings Cost?

At the next meeting you attend, spend a few moments estimating its cost. You will need to include:

■ Salaries

■ Administration costs before and after the meeting

■ Travel expenses

■ Equipment costs or hiring charges

- Venue charges

- Stationery, printing, postage

- Telephone charges (before or, in a teleconference, during the meeting)

- Refreshments

- Lost opportunity costs (while sales staff are not selling, for example)

Look at the figure you have come up with (it's unlikely to be less than a few hundred pounds per hour). Ask yourself: does the cost reflect the quality of discussion and decision making in the meeting?

Research suggests that there will be a 5 – 9% rise in the frequency of meetings over the next five years.

Peter Honey, the occupational psychologist, estimates that up to 60% of senior managers' time is spent in meetings. Yet a recent survey found that 72% of those same managers considered the meetings they attended a waste of time.

As J.K. Galbraith once remarked: *'Meetings are indispensable when you don't want to do anything.'*

So:

Why Have Meetings?

There are a number of powerful reasons for holding meetings.

To bring people together

Humans are gregarious. There are very few people who can get through a day comfortably without interacting with others.

We like to meet: especially in work situations which tend to isolate us from each other. Meetings help us to relate what we are doing to the work of others.

To evaluate information

A meeting is not usually the most efficient way to disseminate information; but it is a good means of evaluating it. A group's judgement is generally more balanced than that of an individual: as a result, groups tend to make fewer gross errors. They are therefore better placed:

To make decisions

The best meetings are called to promote action; to respond to change; to resolve disagreements; to decide between alternative courses of action. Groups are not good at analysing problems which need expert knowledge or subtle reasoning: in both cases a group will think only as well as its most competent member. A decision made by a meeting will carry more weight than one made by an individual: but it will be made more slowly and expensively.

To inspire

Groups that set their own goals often make higher demands for themselves than their superiors might consider practical. The support of the group energizes and motivates individuals to perform better.

Why Meetings Fail

Meetings are natural events: which is why their failure is felt so keenly. An unsuccessful meeting may do more harm than one which never happens.

There are numerous reasons why meetings fail:

The meeting is unnecessary

The job could be done in some simpler, cheaper way; it is routine and does not need to be discussed; information can be transmitted on paper or electronically;

only one or two people need to be involved; or the problem needs the attention of a single expert. Perhaps there is nothing to be done at all!

The meeting is held for the wrong reason

Managers often call meetings merely to wield power over others, or to pursue some private agenda. They use the meeting to rubberstamp decisions – or as a steamroller. Sometimes they are frightened of taking a difficult decision and use the meeting as protection.

Many meetings happen as a matter of habit: a habit which nobody dares challenge. Or they are primarily social occasions: a chance to 'get away from the desk'. Meetings of this kind are group therapy in disguise: they are held to avoid loneliness.

The objective of the meeting is unclear

Nobody has asked why the meeting is being held. Nobody has been informed of its purpose; they have not received or read any of the supporting papers. The agenda is vague and unhelpful; or doesn't exist.

The wrong people are there

Nobody present has the authority to make the required decisions.

Or the right people are absent: substitutes are sent at the last minute, who are ill-informed and unable to take responsibility.

Lack of proper control

The procedure of the meeting is unclear; timekeeping is appalling; the discussion rambles from point to point; hidden agendas hijack the proceedings; conflict, when it occurs, is not properly managed.

Blame for any or all of these problems is usually laid at the feet of a weak Chair; but a dictatorial Chair, who represses discussion rather than controlling it, can be just as damaging.

Poor environment

The venue is inappropriate or uncomfortable; facilities are poor; disruptions destroy concentration.

Poor timing

It's the wrong time of day/week/month/year to make the decision; the meeting fails to start or end on time; people arrive late or leave early.

Poor decision making

The group has inadequate information – or too much information, which creates confusion. The group may be too large to create consensus, or too small to allow adequate debate. The meeting breaks up without agreement. Nothing is done: or, in an effort to give the impression that something has been achieved, the group agrees to more meetings!

How to Make Meetings Work

Meetings will not improve by magic. People must want change, and be willing to implement it.

Altering the way a group of people behaves can be difficult. Sometimes only a policy decision will do the trick. A senior manager in a large transport company recently issued an edict banning all meetings on Fridays, so that staff would be at their desks at least one day a week.

Even if change is not implemented systematically, everybody can change their own behaviour and affect the progress of the meetings they attend. The longest journey starts with a single step: and somebody has to take it. Why not you?

This book is about how to conduct meetings for everybody's benefit. It is not about how to manipulate them or subvert them. It is based on a few golden rules:

- Every meeting is unique.

- A meeting's success is judged by the actions that result from it.

- Running a meeting is the responsibility of the whole group.

2

Before the Meeting

Ninety per cent of an effective meeting happens before it takes place.

We have all been victims of the impromptu meeting. A colleague puts their head round the door and asks: *'Can you pop in for a moment?'* We have no idea why; we are quite unable to prepare. Maybe even they don't know why they want to meet, exactly. If only they had given the matter a moment's thought; if only we had asked...

Any meeting, even the briefest or most informal, will benefit from preparation, if only a few notes scribbled on the back of an envelope. A more formal meeting, involving more than a few people, *must* be organized thoroughly.

The Chair: Setting the Agenda

Every meeting has an agenda. It may not have been written down; it may not have been discussed or even thought about. But the agenda is there, all the same. Whoever controls the agenda controls the meeting. If the agenda is not made public, the meeting will be hijacked by private agendas: the result will be confusion, frustration and failure.

A written agenda allows everyone to focus on what they are to do: before, during and after the meeting. It acts as:

- a plan of the meeting to aid preparation;

- an objective control of the meeting's progress;

- a measure of the meeting's success.

The responsibility for setting the agenda of the meeting is the Chair's. After all, you're calling it.

You must also involve the Adminstrator in your preparation. You will not be able to function efficiently unless you delegate the administration of the meeting; the Administrator will not be able to contribute fully if they are not kept in the picture.

Chair and Administrator should hold a pre-meeting meeting to clarify a series of basic points: Why? Who? Where? When? What? How?

Keep it simple. The more difficult it is to organize, the greater the likelihood that the meeting will be unproductive.

Why are we meeting?

Establish the purpose of the meeting. Write it down: this will form the basis of the meeting's title. *'This meeting is being called in order to...'* Your statement of purpose should revolve around a verb. What are you going to do – apart from talk?

If you are going to address a number of tasks, they should be connected in some way. Are they all relevant to all the members of the group? Is the meeting necessary to carry them all out? Some tasks might be dealt with more efficiently in 'mini-meetings' before or after the main meeting, without wasting the group's time.

What do you want to achieve? Perhaps you will need to consider:

■ the ideal outcome;

■ the realistic outcome;

■ a fallback position.

What decisions will be taken? Will the meeting have the authority to take them? Are resources available to carry out any actions you anticipate? Is anybody else going to be affected? Should they be consulted – or invited to the meeting?

Finally, ask yourself: *what makes this meeting different from the last meeting?* If you can't tell, you haven't yet clarified the meeting's objective.

Who is involved?

The meeting's purpose will govern who attends.

Are they the right people? What is their relevance to the purpose of the meeting? Perhaps they are:

- key decision makers;

- experts or givers of information;

- people who need the information;

- opinion formers;

- senior managers with an interest in the decisions to be reached;

- arbitrators in potential disputes;

- friends, consultants or guests.

Do they represent a wide range of opinions or skills? Discussion (even disagreement) is, after all, the reason why the meeting is being held.

Are they able to attend? The more valuable they are to the meeting, the less likely they are to be available! Will a deputy or last minute substitute be acceptable?

Do they form a natural group? They will certainly act as a group the moment they are sitting round the table – either happily or not. How well do they know each other? Do they have shared concerns, attitudes or philosophies? What are their interests, aims, ambitions, or assumptions about each other? Are all of these individual attitudes and interests reconcilable within the group? Where is the common ground between them?

How many people will attend? Remember the famous saying: '*The usefulness of a meeting is in inverse proportion to the numbers attending.'* Fewer people working for longer will be more productive than more people working quickly. Large groups are always in danger of splitting into sub-groups – either into the speakers and the silent, or into alliances ranged against one another.

HOW MANY IS ENOUGH?

	Advantages	Disadvantages
Small Groups (2–5)	Cohesive High productivity All participants visible Low absenteeism Less danger of cliques	Narrow range of skills Difficult to generate discussion Unreliable decisions Danger of social occasion
Large groups (10+)	Sound decisions Lots of points of view Group pressure on saboteurs	Difficult to get consensus Need for more control People scared into silence High absenteeism Meetings within the meeting Danger of cliques forming

The ideal number for an internal business meeting is between six and nine:

- a group of this size has a high productivity rate;

- individuals are not swallowed up in the crowd;

- cliques are less likely to form;

- the group is easier to control.

What do the Participants need in order to prepare for the meeting? Should you brief them or send them papers: the minutes of the last meeting, reports, the latest data? Can we be sure that they will read the papers before the meeting?

Where are we meeting?

Is the venue conveniently located? Is it accessible: for people with disabilities, for example, or women travelling alone at night?

Are you meeting on 'home ground'? Will everybody feel at ease when they are there – or will they be intimidated by the trophies of a dominant senior manager? If the meeting is being held in a hotel or conference venue, you will need to liaise to establish timings, numbers, catering and needs for equipment. Is the room the right size and shape? Is it suitable for your purpose? Consider:

- acoustics;

- heating, lighting and ventilation;

- chairs – quantity and comfort;

- tables – size, flexibility and sturdiness;

- equipment and power points;

- procedures – fire drill, refreshments, toilets, messages, telephones;

- distractions – air-conditioning, trains, noise, the view, building work, intercoms.

PLANNING THE ROOM LAYOUT

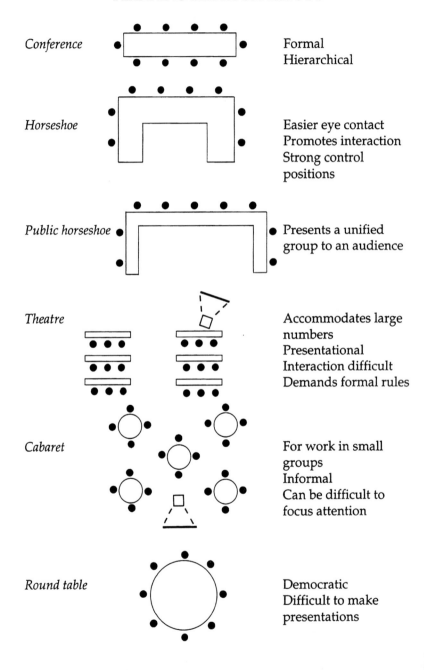

Conference — Formal / Hierarchical

Horseshoe — Easier eye contact / Promotes interaction / Strong control positions

Public horseshoe — Presents a unified group to an audience

Theatre — Accommodates large numbers / Presentational / Interaction difficult / Demands formal rules

Cabaret — For work in small groups / Informal / Can be difficult to focus attention

Round table — Democratic / Difficult to make presentations

Ask whether furniture and fittings are:

■ fixed – walls, windows, doors?

■ semi-fixed – partitions, seating, projection screens, white boards?

■ moveable – chairs, tables, equipment?

Be careful not to regard semi-fixed fittings as fixed! You may lose an opportunity to adapt a room better to your needs.

The layout of furniture will be governed by the style of the meeting. The Chair may wish to place allies (or potential troublemakers!) in 'control positions'; the Administrator will need to be able to communicate easily with everybody while taking the minutes. If presentations are to be given, everybody should be able to see a screen or flip chart with a minimum of disruption.

Participants should be about one arm's length from each other. Closer, they will invade each other's space; further apart, they will feel isolated and the group dynamics will suffer. Remember, too, that effective interaction depends on easy eye contact.

When is the meeting being held? (and when will it end?)

Is the date of the meeting auspicious? Can everybody attend? Is it close enough to register in people's memories, and far enough ahead to allow them to prepare? Is it a 'good' day of the week?

Everybody knows that some times of the day are better than others for alertness. Ergonomic research suggests that the best time for making decisions is late morning: a finding confirmed by the international air company who made it policy for all meetings to be held in one of two slots: 0900–1100 and 1100–1300. Meeting at the end of the day might spur people to make rapid decisions; but they may not make good ones.

Are your meetings too long? It is a recurrent complaint. Some Chairs seem to make it a point of honour to have meetings that last for hours. But longer doesn't mean better. To quote John deButts, Chairman of American Telephone and Telegraph: *'A successful meeting depends on how much everybody participates, not on how long it is.'* No meeting, or part of a meeting, should extend beyond 90 minutes. If you must go on longer, include time for breaks, refreshment, or meals.

MAKING MEETINGS SHORTER

- Announce a finishing time. It's discourteous and dangerous not to.
- Limited the number of items on the agenda to the time allowed.
- Give a time limit to each agenda item.
- Allow time for breaks.
- Prepare procedures for unresolved business.
- Make your goal: to end on time!

Meetings are often overlong because they have no scheduled time to end. 'We just go on until we've finished', sighs the beleaguered Chair. Nothing does more harm to concentration and discipline than an open-ended meeting. The agenda should announce a finishing time – and the Chair should make sure that it is kept to.

What goes on the agenda?

The most formal of agendas will include:

- Title of meeting

- Date, time, venue

- Apologies for absence

- Minutes of previous meeting

- Matters arising from the previous meeting

- Other items to be discussed and decided

- Motions relating to the above

- Reports from sub-committees

- Contributions from guest speakers

- Any other business

- Date, time and venue of next meeting

The agenda should indicate what will happen at the meeting. Each item is a task: its title on the agenda should indicate what the task is and how it will be tackled.

Every item on the agenda, therefore, should contain at least one verb, indicating what the group will do.

'Item 3: New IT network.' – says very little that will help Participants to prepare. Compare:

'Item 3: New IT network.

Clive to present quotations and essential specifications of systemts under consideration. Team to agree system to be recommended for purchase.'

As you gather items for the agenda, look for:

- a logical order;

- a common thread: keep linked items together;

- routine items;

ASSEMBLING THE AGENDA

- Remove any unncecessary items.

- Give detailed titles to each item.

- Every title should contain at least one verb: what the group will do.

- Give timings to each item.

- Indicate any specific speakers to an item.

- Note any attached papers – in case of loss.

- Consider putting motions on a separate sheet, for ease of reference.

- special factors (Participants who are only involved in a small part of the meeting; people who have to arrive late or leave early);

- difficult or contentious items;

- a balance between urgent and important items.

The agenda should follow a natural shape: the most 'difficult' items – those needing the most discussion and work – will be best placed in the middle third of the meeting, when the group's physical and mental alertness are at their peak. Routine items, or urgent matters which can be dealt with quickly, can be put first; and the 'easiest' items – those of greatest interest, or presentations by guest speakers – towards the end.

PLANNING AN AGENDA
(with Acknowledgements to D. Sharman, *The Perfect Meeting*)

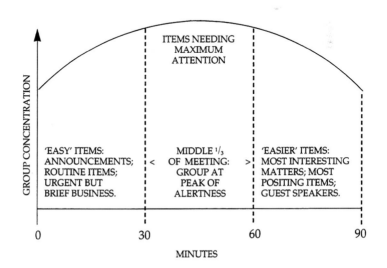

The more you try to pack onto your agenda, the less you'll achieve. Always look for unnecessary items, which can be dealt with outside the meeting.

Beware Any Other Business! It is a timebomb ticking away beneath the meeting, ready to explode at the last minute. Old scores are settled, old grudges resurface, lengthy and irrelevant complaints sabotage the group's achievement.

If something is worth discussing, it should be on the agenda. If a sudden critical problem arises, there should be a procedure for altering the agenda at the last moment: at the Chair's discretion. Otherwise, the matter should await the next meeting.

HOW TO AVOID 'ANY OTHER BUSINESS'

1. Distribute a draft agenda, with invitations for contributions.

2. Any Participant with late business must contact the Chair or Administrator before the meeting starts.

3. Any late inclusions are at the Chair's discretion.

4. At the start of the meeting, the Chair indicates any alterations to the agenda – with revised timings.

5. Nothing else is allowed in that meeting.

How will the meeting be run?

What type of meeting are you holding? Does it have regulations or legal requirements governing the way it's run? How do you expect Participants to contribute? How will you control procedure? Will everybody address their remarks formally through the Chair? Perhaps you will opt for a strategy of minimal control: announcing each item, summarizing discussion, calling for a formal decision – and keeping to time. The group will perform more effectively if they are assured that the procedure of the meeting is under control.

The Administrator's Role

The Administrator should have been involved in – or at the very least informed of – all the Chair's preparations. You should know:

- the purpose of the meeting;

- who is attending;

- what will go on the agenda, and the purpose of each item;

- background information to help you take the minutes.

How will the meeting's progress be recorded? Don't be hidebound by tradition: consider how the minutes of the meeting can be improved. The task of taking minutes will be made easier if you have the authority to:

- intervene to clarify points that are unclear;

- summarize at the end of each item with details of decisions and actions agreed.

You can also be invaluable in helping to keep time. Discuss these matters with the Chair. If you establish your responsibilities at this stage, your work during the meeting will be more rewarding.

Now your tasks are:

■ **To send notice of the meeting to all Participants**
The agenda will need to be distributed, perhaps in draft form with invitations for contributions. If they have not already been distributed, you may also send the minutes of the last meeting (so that you won't have to read them in the meeting!).

■ **To liaise with Participants**
Can they attend? Do they need travel instructions? They may have papers they want prepared and distributed. If they are making a presentation, they may want you to provide equipment.

■ **To prepare documents**
People may need to be chased for manuscripts. Reports must be prepared, copied and distributed.

■ **To arrange the booking and preparation of the room**
Sometimes more easily said than done!

■ **To arrange any equipment that is needed**
Make sure you know where to go for help in the event of a breakdown.

■ **To arrange refreshments**
Check any special dietary requirements, and that catering staff are aware of your break times.

You should arrive at the meeting amply prepared. Possible needs will include:

- Spare agendas (or revised agendas)
- Spare copies of all supporting papers
- Notepaper
- Flipchart paper and pens
- Stapler and paper clips
- Pens and pencils
- List of participants
- Name cards
- Badges
- Rule book (in case of procedural squabbles!)

A TIMETABLE FOR MEETING ADMINISTRATION

Task	Day	Action
Notice of meeting	–10	Chair/Administrator
Submission of draft items and papers	–8	Participants
Agenda agreed and distributed	–7	Chair/Administrator
Day of meeting	0	All
First draft of minutes to Chair	+2	Administrator
Minutes approved and distributed	+4	Chair/Administrator

Preparation for Participants

British managers have a reputation for arriving at meetings unprepared. The interplay of ideas at the meeting itself is certainly important: but your performance will benefit enormously from a little careful forethought.

■ Find out the meeting's purpose

Make it your business to know what the meeting's about. Read the agenda. Check anything you don't understand – particularly if your name is beside it!

■ Read the distributed papers

There is no excuse for not doing so, if they've been sent in good time.

■ Prepare your contribution

What contribution will you make? Inform the Chair of any item you want included – in good time – and how you would like to participate. Make notes of specific points you will raise against any item. If you are making a formal presentation, it will need detailed preparation; perhaps the Administrator will need to be informed of any equipment you will need.

What role are you expected to play? The Chair – or other Participants – may see you as:

- an ideas person: the expert;
- a doer: who will take action;
- a sounding board for others' suggestions;
- a mediator;
- a representative of your team or department.
- Defined roles can help people to communicate and make relationships within the group more stable.

■ Identify your private agenda

Everybody goes to meetings with private agendas. They may emerge at some point; they may be forced into the open; they may remain forever hidden. There is nothing wrong with a private agenda, if it is conceived constructively and positively.

Good private agendas might include:

- seeing the meeting as a career investment;

- helping the Chair achieve a successful meeting;

- strengthening the group;

- encouraging other Participants;

- gaining agreement for your own plans.

Bad private agendas will include:

- wanting to please;

- empire building;

- wanting to conform;

- venting your frustration;

- causing conflict;

- discrediting a rival;

- undermining the Chair;

- scoring points off others;

- riding a favourite hobbyhorse;

- demonstrating how overworked you are (*'Poor me'*...).

Identify your private agenda. Ask yourself honestly whether it's worthwhile or professional – and how it will appear if it's unmasked. It should never take over the meeting. Prepare to operate in the space between the agendas, public and private.

3

During the Meeting

A meeting is a group in action. To understand how to get the best from a meeting, we need to know a little of how people behave when they gather together.

How Groups Work

Groups have their own rules. They operate according to the principles of synergy: originally a biological term for the correlation of groups of organs in the body to perform a single function, and hence an expression of the collective energy of a group of people.

The essence of synergy is that the whole is greater than the sum of its parts: collective knowledge is greater than that of individuals because extra information is generated within the group; and collective action will be more productive because the group motivates itself to a higher degree.

A group's first task is to survive. From the moment it begins to form, it works to strengthen itself. If counteracting forces are too strong and the group splinters, other groups will at once begin to form.

Individuals' primary aim within the group is to be accepted: to integrate. They will pursue the essential aims of:

- well-being (physical, mental, emotional, economic, spiritual);
- a sense of belonging;
- recognition from the group;
- control over their own lives.

If the behaviour of the group satisfies these needs, the individual will respond by strengthening the group.

Four stages of group behaviour have been identified by occupational psychologists:

Forming

A group is newly constructed: individuals are in a tentative relationship to each other. Anxiety. The group leader must quickly strengthen the group by identifying what binds it together, and by stating the rules for its behaviour.

Storming

Individuals may rebel against the leader or each other;

the group, however, wants to survive. Gradually it will begin to resolve this conflict by applying pressure on any who challenge the strongest claim to the group's identity: first by reason; then by emotional pressure; then by threats of isolation; and finally by rejection.

Those who conform will internalize the group's values and label non-conformists as 'dissidents'.

Norming

The group finds a common set of values. This allows for a freer exchange of views. Conflict is acknowledged and allowed within strict bounds, or suppressed in the interests of group harmony. A sense of the team emerges.

Performing

The group works towards a common goal, reaching decisions by consensus and acting as one unit.

A group may bounce back and forth between these states during one meeting. Groups are naturally conservative and resist any change which threatens their cohesion. 'Boardroom battles' are often the stormy responses of highly conservative groups to inevitable change.

Chairing the Meeting

The Chair's task is to use the talents of the group: to release the potential latent in the people around the table. How this is achieved will depend very much on the style that the Chair finds congenial; but experience suggests that clear control of the process of the meeting – the rules by which it is conducted – will allow the group to accomplish their tasks more creatively.

Opening the meeting

A meeting which starts badly will take time to recover. It's a good idea for the Chair to work out an opening procedure in some detail: it will steady the nerves and put everybody at ease. People may need to be introduced; the purpose of the meeting will have to be made clear. Above all, the group should be made to feel welcome.

■ Start on time

If you don't, you'll have late arrivals for the next meeting.

Anybody who arrives late at a meeting which started promptly will soon get the message.

■ State the purpose or objective of the meeting

Refer to the agenda, and indicate the common ground that exists within the group to reach this goal.

■ Make all suitable introductions

Check that everybody knows each other. Attend in particular to new members.

■ Announce procedures and the timetable of the meeting

Tell people how long the meeting will last, and times of breaks. Indicate how you expect them to contribute; how decisions will be reached (by consensus; by voting); and how discussion will be controlled.

■ If you are chairing a new group:

identify and agree the group's purpose; give information on everybody attending: their expertise and relevance to the task; and invite everybody to introduce themselves.

■ If the group is well established:

identify the purpose of this meeting; note any changes in circumstances since the last meeting; remind the group of its identity; introduce new members or guests; and praise achievements of group/individuals since the last meeting; acknowledge new difficulties; and reaffirm the determination of the meeting to meet the challenge.

Keeping control

One of the most common criticisms of Chairs is that they fail to control the meeting. Another is that they are too autocratic!

Strict control must be exercised at the start of the meeting, when a group is newly formed, or when the meeting is large and a high degree of procedural discipline must be invoked. 'Strong' control is useful in a crisis, or to get through routine items quickly.

Otherwise a democratic style is to be preferred. Groups work best when they feel ownership of the tasks to be undertaken, and empowered to act. They will also work more efficiently if they feel secure and that somebody is in overall control.

■ Keep control of the task

Stick to the agenda. Disallow irrelevancy and bring the discussion back to the point by summarizing and asking questions. If you must deviate from the agenda, explain exactly why and how you will do so. Always search for common ground so that the task is owned by the whole group. Be ready to handle emotional outbursts by referring back to the task in hand. Clarify decisions and actions to be taken.

■ Keep control of the procedure

Establish the rules and stick to them. Procedures should be simple, so that everybody can understand and operate them; and flexible, to allow for maximum participation. Keep to time. Make the rules clear from the start, but be prepared to adjust your style to the group. Expect the unexpected – late arrivals, early departures.

The best Chairs wear their authority lightly. The writer of the Tao Te Ching recognized this over 2,000 years ago:

The best soldier is not soldierly
The best fighter is not ferocious
The best conqueror does not take part in the war
The best employer of men keeps himself below them
This is called the virtue of not contending
This is called the ability of using men

– *and women!*

Discussing each item

Each item should be dealt with separately, and in order. The Chair should also present each item positively. Don't ask 'What went wrong?' and invite old complaints and conflicts. Ask instead: 'What shall we do to solve the problem?'

- Refer to the agenda

- Don't start an item before concluding the previous one

- Clarify the purpose of the item

- Start the discussion positively

- Remind the group how much time is allocated

- Give any relevant background information

- Try to change your approach a little from item to

item: invite someone to begin or throw the discussion open to the whole group

Encouraging contributions

The purpose of the meeting is to exchange ideas. An important idea may never be expressed because somebody is too reticent – or overawed – to volunteer it. The meeting becomes a tennis match: ideas are bounced back and forth between a few dominant personalities and everybody else looks on helplessly.

The Chair can encourage democracy in two ways:

- Task behaviour: initiating discussion, building on it, making suggestions, urging the group on;

- Process behaviour: gate-keeping to allow everyone to contribute; time-keeping to concentrate people's minds; and summarizing the group's feelings.

Everybody should feel relaxed about contributing, and that their contribution is valued.

- **Always ask for different points of view**

- **Allow debate**

- **Note who is not talking and make space for them to contribute**

- **Separate creative contributions from critical ones: less assertive Participants will be encouraged to contribute**

Questions and statements

Use these to guide the discussion; to open it, keep it alive, or bring it to a close. Use questions to encourage people to speak from their experience or expertise, or to contribute to the discussion without seeming to lose your impartiality.

TYPES OF QUESTION

CLOSED (Can only be answered 'yes' or 'no')	*'Have you brought the figures with you?'*	To establish facts. To focus discussion. To stop rambling.
OPEN (Cannot be answered 'yes' or 'no')	*'What do you think of this proposal?'*	To open or widen the discussion. To get ideas as well as facts.
SPECIFIC	*'When did the fault occur?'*	Directs the discussion. Pins the speaker down.
OVERHEAD	*'Can we agree on what we need?'*	Addresses the group as a whole. Makes a point without sacrificing impartiality.
RELAY	*'Thanks Gill. John, what do you think about this?'*	From one speaker to another.
REVERSE	*'Well: what do you think?'*	Reflects a question or statement back to the speaker.

Statements are useful for introducing a subject:

'We're all aware of the problems in this area. They include. . .'

■ to give information:

'This is a new venture for the company. Briefly it works like this. . .'

■ to temper emotion with fact:

'Perhaps I can make a few points clear at this stage.'

■ or to gauge the mood of the group:

'I can see that there's a good deal of frustration about this.'

'I think we're all satisfied about that decision.'

'It seems to me that we're getting confused.'

Summarizing

All meetings go through periods of relative calm: between or within items. The group is uncertain of the next move. Discussion dries up, begins to go in circles, or degenerates into chat. At times like this, the Chair should intervene with a summary.

Good timing is essential. Don't try to summarize when the discussion is in full swing: take notes instead to prepare yourself for the moment when the group stops generating ideas.

Summarizing within items

Control contributions by summarizing them – when they ramble, repeat themselves or become anecdotal.

Mark the end of one phase of the discussion with a summary before inviting further comments.

Summarize to bring together the strands of a discussion, or to revive it when it goes slack.

Summarizing at the end of items

Mark the end of the discussion with a summary of what has been covered, and to clarify exactly what has been agreed.

This is a task that can usefully be given to the minute-taker, to help prepare the minutes.

Summarizing at the end of the meeting

A brief summary will remind the group of its achievement and point the way forward to the actions that will be taken.

Closing the meeting

Closing is as important as opening. The group is about to break up: its identity must be reaffirmed so that the sense of a team persists.

- **Summarize what has been decided and point the way ahead**

- **Briefly announce what actions are to occur: by whom, and when**

- **End positively. Emphasize the results of the meeting**

- **Thank everybody for their attendance and their contributions**

The Administrator as Minute-taker

Minutes are:

- a reminder of what happened at the meeting;
- a basis for discussion of matters arising at the next meeting;
- a guide for non-attendees;
- a permanent record.

Taking minutes during the meeting involves two skills: listening and note-taking.

Listening

In a society that communicates increasingly through visual images, listening has become a highly complex and much underrated skill. Most people in meetings will be thinking and speaking at the same time. Sometimes they will all be talking at once!

Only a small proportion of the words we use carries the objective information we wish to communicate. Most people surround their thoughts with words which express feelings, attitudes to the listeners or their relationship to the group. It requires concentration to edit the important points from the surrounding verbiage.

- **Listen for facts and ideas, not merely to the words**
- **Listen for actions: performed, suggested or agreed**
- **Identify references to change**
- **Intervene to clarify a point that's unclear**

- Ask if you don't know what has been decided, or what action will be taken

- Summarize each item from your minute notes before moving to the next

---

SUMMARIZING A DISCUSSION

- What has happened? Who has been responsible?

- What has not been done?

- What has changed since the last meeting?

- What must be done?

- What decision has been taken?

- Are there serious disagreements? By whom? On what grounds?

- What action will be taken? When? Where? By whom?

Note-taking

You cannot listen and take notes at the same time. Your primary task is to understand what is going on: most of your time in the meeting should be spent listening. You should take notes only intermittently.

Beware shorthand. It will tempt you to record what is said, rather than what is thought. Your task is to note ideas, facts, decisions and actions. Your notes should make these clear at once.

The trick is to be able to note down only keywords. The danger is that you will only record pieces of information in isolation: when you return to your notes, you may have no idea why you have noted them. What is it about this information that makes it relevant? What has happened? What has changed?

There are a number of common ways of taking minutes. Use a method which you find comfortable.

PAGE FROM A COLUMN-STYLE MINUTE BOOK

NAME	INFO	ACTION
BRIAN	ITEM 6 Finance systems must be reviewed John Wright to investigate Report to fin. management team	J.W. 6.4.95

A **minute book**, hard-backed and A4 size, works like this:

- Each page is ruled into three columns: the central one half a page width.

- Column 1 for the names of speakers;
  Column 2 for keywords: decisions and actions;
  Column 3 for names of people taking action, and a 'by when' date.

The narrow central column dissuades you from writing too much. Actions are clearly highlighted. Leave space at the end of each item for late additions.

Pattern plans are a very effective method of note-taking.

- Use plain paper, at least A4 size. One sheet per agenda item. Put the number and title of the item in a circle in the middle of the page.

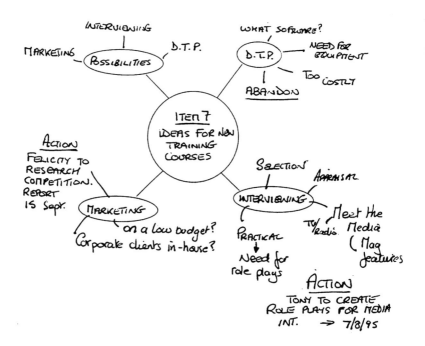

- Note down each idea as it is mentioned, with the initials of the speaker if necessary. Give the ideas lots of space and add related comments as they arise in the appropriate part of the plan.

- Use boxes for decisions, agreed actions, and information to be forwarded to non-attendees.

Pattern plans have a number of clear advantages. They allow you to follow the course of the discussion – no matter where it goes! Because the paper is plain and you are writing in a 'field' rather than along lines, you are forced to listen creatively for key ideas and the connections between them. You cannot slip into writing sentences or recording dialogue because there is no room. Your material organizes itself as it is recorded. Your final note will be brief, structured and highly focussed: writing up the minutes will be far quicker and easier.

Participating Well

Everybody is responsible for the success of the meeting. Preparation, punctuality and politeness are essential. But participating well is more than doing the bare minimum.

■ Arrive on time
You owe it to others and to yourself. If you are held up, try to get a message through.

■ Concentrate
Look at other speakers. Take notes. Fight the distractions to good listening: pondering what has just

been said; thinking about what you want to say; getting emotional; interruptions; hunger or thirst; daydreaming. If concentration flags: pretend to listen! It will help you to concentrate for real.

■ Be open-minded
Listen to what is said: not what you'd like to hear. Don't dismiss ideas out of hand. What can you contribute to somebody else's idea to improve it?

■ Help the progress of the meeting
Support the Chair. Appeal to the agenda to help keep order – and time. Keep your remarks to the point. Be a good gate-keeper, encouraging others to contribute. Ask for clarification. Be ready to summarize what has been achieved so far; particularly if it's not very much!

■ Be polite and patient
It may not be easy to hold your tongue; but others have the same right to speak as you.

IT'S NO GOOD, BRIAN –
THE VOTE WENT
AGAINST YOU.

- **Accept the decisions reached by due process**
The essence of democracy.

Speaking in Meetings

The progress of your career may depend on how well you speak in meetings. You can demonstrate the incisiveness of your ideas, your understanding of the way things work, and your willingness to contribute positively. This is your chance to be noticed.

Note down what you want to say, before and during the meeting. Written notes will focus your mind. Demonstrating that you've prepared – by leaning forward and picking up your notes – is extraordinarily effective for gaining the meeting's attention. Here at least, you are saying, is someone who knows what they want to say. Here is someone who means business.

- **Speak quickly**
We hear at least four times faster than we speak.

- **Express yourself accurately**
State your main idea immediately, before elaborating. Make one point at a time. Support your opinion with facts: uncontroversial ones, and not too many of them. Beware sweeping generalizations – 'always', 'never', 'everybody'; and try not to qualify your ideas too much with 'on the other hand', 'although of course', 'well not all the time', 'not forgetting'...

- **Raise (and lower) your voice**
Raise your voice in volume, and lower it in pitch. Speak to the people around you: not at the table. Aim

your voice at the person furthest from you. A lower pitch will indicate calmness; shrillness suggests lack of confidence.

■ Look at the whole group

Not the ceiling or the wall above their heads! Catch people's eyes. Don't favour the Chair or one person. Your eyes should scan everybody equally.

JUDGING THE MOMENT TO SPEAK

When is the best time to make your point?

At the start of the discussion

You will be able to 'set the agenda', and establish control of the discussion at once. The danger is that you might lose control later.

In the middle of the discussion

The previous contribution might act as a trigger for your own, a foundation on which your idea can build. It might be directly opposed to yours and so allow you to make a dramatic contrast. Or perhaps it was poorly expressed, incomplete, emotional or off the point, and so give you the advantage.

At the end of the discussion

By waiting patiently for everybody else to tie themselves in knots, you can intervene at the last moment and impress the whole meeting with a flash of clear thinking, briefly expressed. This could give you maximum control over a decision. It's a high risk tactic; but it often works.

- **Keep calm**
  If necessary, hold onto something to keep gestures to a minimum.

- **Be fearless**
  Challenge others' point of views: state your own positively and unequivocally.

Making a Presentation at a Meeting

Making a formal presentation at a business meeting is many people's idea of purgatory. You are on the spot. A lively, friendly group of people suddenly becomes a silent audience, hanging on your every word. You feel that your credibility with your colleagues - or seniors - is at stake.

There are three elements that contribute to the success of any presentation:

- who you are

- what you say

- how you say it

By far the most important of these is the first. You must be yourself.

The great advantage of a presentation is that it allows the speaker to infect the audience with enthusiasm. You have the opportunity to bring the material alive. The formality of the occasion allows you to present a structured case without interruption. But you also have the flexibility to focus on issues which are relevant to the audience and to clarify what may be unclear to them.

75% of what you say will be forgotten within 24 hours. For this reason, presentations are not a good way to give complicated information. The most common fault with business presentations is that the speaker includes far too much detail.

Preparing the presentation

Establish the purpose of your presentation. Virtually all presentations are designed to serve one of three broad purposes:

- to inform;

- to persuade;

- to entertain.

Actually your presentation will probably do a little of all three: what is its main purpose?

Write down a statement of objective. It will clear your mind, help you in the selection of material and act as a check when your preparation is complete.

Give close consideration to your audience:

- What is their status range?

- How many of them are there?

- How well informed are they?

- What do they want from you?

- What is their attitude towards you or your subject?

Remember that your audience will have certain expectations, of you and of itself. It's up to you to fulfil them.

Audience expectations of speaker	Audience expectations of itself
■ To set the direction	■ To be led
■ To set the pace and to maintain it	■ To work at the speaker's pace
■ To be competence and confident	■ To be told what to do

Organizing your material

Your presentation must have a message. You are not merely giving information, but persuading your audience that you are right, that they have something to gain from listening to you, and that they should do what you want them to do.

What are you trying to convey? Sum it up in a single statement. Is it a message that your audience will want to hear? Why should they believe it when you deliver it?

Every topic can be broken down into categories. These will form the core of your presentation. If the audience doesn't remember every detail, they should be able to remember how you categorized your material.

■ **All of your categories should contribute to your message**
Don't include anything that contradicts or detracts from the message. You'll give ammunition to the

audience with which to shoot you down! Let them think of counter-arguments; and be ready to rebut them.

■ **Keep the number of categories small**

We remember items in groups of four or five: no more. If you have a large number of categories, you must simplify by collecting them into larger categories.

■ **Categories must all be of the same kind**

If you are persuading the meeting of the benefits of a new system, each category should be a type of benefit: ease of use, efficiency, congruence with other systems. If you are telling people how to operate the system, each category will be a stage in the procedure.

■ **Give each category a name that will be easily remembered**

Keep them simple. Introduce them at the beginning. Repeat them as you come to each, and again at the end of the presentation.

Opening and closing

The most important parts of the presentation are the beginning and the end. It's a good idea to have these worked out in detail so that they are fail-safe.

The audience will only hear your words once. So, in order to build their recall, you will have to repeat the essential information you want them to remember. The opening and close of your presentation will contain summaries of your message and the main categories into which you have divided the information.

HOW TO OPEN:

■ **Take control**
State your message. Tell the audience how long you will speak for. Tell the audience what you expect of them: whether they should take notes, how you will handle questions.

■ **Acknowledge the audience**
Why is your message relevant to them? How will it benefit them?

■ **Establish your credentials**
What is your expertise? What experience do you have? What have you done as background for this presentation?

■ **Introduce the subject matter**
Explain the purpose of your presentation and the structure that you will follow. Name the main categories.

The audience will now be confident that you know what you are doing. This will allow them to relax and actually listen to you!

HOW TO CLOSE:

■ **Signal that you have finished and are about to wrap up**
This will sharpen your audience's concentration, and prepare them for your final summary.

■ **Restate your message, and the categories you have covered**
This is your last chance to signal the structure of your thinking.

■ **Emphasize actions that you expect to result from your presentation – and the benefits to all.**
Be positive; Re-emphasize your understanding of the audience.

■ **Thank the audience for their attention and invite questions**
You can relax! Show the audience that you are prepared to wait for a moment: keep eye contact.

Visual aids

How will the audience remember what you are telling them? They will recall concrete examples and images much more easily than concepts; but this doesn't mean that every idea must be accompanied by a slide or a slogan on the overhead projector!

Visual aids are designed to support what you are saying, not substitute for it. There are a few golden rules about using them.

■ **Not every idea needs a visual aid to convey it**
Try instead to find ways of making ideas concrete by using examples, analogies or anecdotes. A story can stick in the mind better than a picture.

■ **Visual aids should present information graphically**
The message is conveyed by its shape on the screen: not by the amount of detail you include.

■ **Words are not visual**
If you do put words on a slide, keep them short, simple, and punchy: no more than you would print on a T-shirt. Avoid vague abstractions or reams of text.

■ **Use pictures to convey what can't be conveyed by words alone**
Pictures, diagrams and graphs should tell their message simply, and boldly.

■ **Don't use a visual aid as a crib sheet**
Talk to the audience, not to the screen.

Answering questions

For many people this is the most worrying part of the presentation. Actually, it should be the easy bit!

■ **Tell your audience at the start how you intend to take questions**
The best way is probably to ask for questions to be put only when you've finished.

■ **Don't be embarrassed by an awkward pause**
You must allow time at the beginning of a question session for the audience to change roles. Sometimes a colleague planted with an opening question is a useful way to get the ball rolling.

■ **Treat all questions as public**
Don't allow yourself to get into a private conversation. Repeat questions which may have been inaudible to the rest of the audience: answer to the whole audience. Keep your answers brief.

■ **If you don't know the answer: say so**
Your authority will be enhanced by your honesty. Offer to find the answer later if appropriate: but don't try to bluff. There is almost bound to be somebody in the audience who does know the answer, and your credibility will be in tatters if they correct you.

Non-Verbal Communication

The non-verbal messages we transmit are far more powerful than the actual words we use. We are all good at observing non-verbal communication accurately; it is worth trying to use it well to help us communicate more effectively in meetings.

Non-verbal communication can be broken down into two areas:

■ Eyes;

■ Body language.

In both cases there are things that are worth looking for in others, and things that we can cultivate for our own benefit: whether as Chair, Administrator or Participant.

Eyes

What to look for in others:

■ **Gazing at the ceiling**
Is it because they are thinking? Or bored? Or exasperated? Or worried about the light fitting?

■ **Somebody hiding their eyes with their hand**
They may be concealing something else. Is is laughter? Tears? Exhaustion? Or eye strain?

■ **Gazing fixedly at the table**
This suggests embarrassment, or trying to avoid being picked on.

■ **Gazing fixedly at someone else**
This could mean anything.

What to do:

- **Ask someone to speak by catching their eye**
- **Seek agreement from the group by encompassing everyone in your gaze**
- **A fierce glance is useful for cautioning or disciplining somebody without causing embarrassment**
- **Looking at a speaker demonstrates that you are paying attention**

Body language

What to look for in others:

- **Leaning forward**
This suggests concentration and engagement. Leaning back could indicate disagreement or an unwillingness to become involved.

- **Arm movements.**
Scratching an ear, playing with hair, hands on head, rubbing the temples – all suggest different responses to what is happening.

- **Shifting feet**
This might indicate boredom or physical discomfort: time for a break! Jiggling a foot can suggest annoyance or lapse of concentration.

- **Fidgeting and doodling**
Sure signs that concentration is flagging.

- **Moments of maximum concentration**
A stillness suddenly takes over the meeting. You

could hear a pin drop. Has a hidden agenda unwittingly been referred to?

What to do:

- **Dress appropriately**

- **Sit comfortably: don't slouch or tie your legs in knots**

- **If you are standing: stand at ease**

- **Keep your hands visible on the table, and still**

- **Keep your hands away from your face: especially when speaking**

- **Lean forward to demonstrate your engagement with the discussion**

Problem People and How to Deal with Them

Every meeting has them. A person will be a problem if their own interests are in open conflict with those of the group. Dealing with them is everybody's responsibility.

A basic rule is always to treat them as group members, not as troublesome individuals. This may be easier said than done!

The bulldog
Aggressive. Inflexible.
Looking for a fight.
Out to score points.
Liable to attack without warning.
Give him a bone to chew.
Separate what he says
from the way he says it.
Keep cool.

The horse
Keen but boring. Goes
by the book.
Intelligent but could
plod on for ever.
Lead them to water:
give them a job to do.
Harness their remarks
by summarizing and restating.

The fox
Crafty. Undermine the meeting.
Whispers a lot.
A potential hijacker.
Force them to make their
conspiratorial view public.
Look for the hidden agenda.
Set the bulldog on them.

The monkey
Know it all: the point-of-order
expert.
Chatters incessantly.
Astute but swings from tree
to tree. Volunteers a lot.
Keep control of procedure.
Ask closed questions.
Give them something
difficult to do.

The hedgehog
Prickly. Whines and whinges.
Tickle their bellies.
Respect their expertise.
Despises everyone else: probably
having been squashed once or
twice.
Sceptical. Unhelpful.
Defensive: tendency to curl up in a
ball.
Ask them to help.
Give them status by giving
responsibility. And a bowl of
warm milk.

The gazelle
Timid and retiring. May be young.
Liable to run away.
A silent worrier.
Unwilling to stand their ground.
Ask direct questions that they can
answer.
Encourage and praise them.

The frog
Blabbermouth. Leaps in
unthinkingly.
'Read it, read it.'
Ill-informed.
Puts his foot in it: the fox's victim.
Keep to the point.
Appeal to the clock.
Ignore gaffes.
Ask them to do the minutes.

The hippo
Wallows.
Half asleep most of the time.
Likes mud. And not much else.
Will agree to anything.
Likely to say: "Why me?"
Try to heave them out.
Pick on them suddenly.
Challenge them.

The giraffe
Easily distracted.
Dreams in the treetops.
Rather sensitive.
Will do anything not to fall over.
Encourage them to come down to earth.
Show respect.
Don't trip them.

Problem Situations and How to Handle Them

The meeting that goes exactly according to plan is a rare event. If the Chair is acting professionally, there should be few situations that cause major disruption. These are perhaps the most serious and the most common.

Loss of direction

Perhaps you're having too much fun! Meetings are always vulnerable to becoming social occasions; discussion can easily descend into 'chat'.

The Chair must refocus. If they are not doing so, a Participant should quietly indicate that the meeting has gone off track. Restate the task; summarize the main ideas so far; ask specific questions. Invoke the clock.

Hijacking

A severe loss of direction, which occurs when a private agenda attempts to take over. It may even involve a conspiracy.

The Chair and other Participants have a duty to rescue the meeting from being hijacked. Alliances may need to be made and appeals made to the agenda. A period of 'storming' may ensue. But a hijack by definition is by one person or a minority. Appeals to group solidarity should be sufficient to solve the problem, at least temporarily. An attempted hijack usually means that a major issue needs to be addressed – though perhaps not at this meeting.

Senior management at meetings chaired by subordinates are prone to hijack. The Chair must try to exercise proper authority. If they conduct the meeting properly and fairly, they will have nothing to fear from a responsible senior manager – who may after all be assessing their leadership potential.

Conflict

Well, some conflict is necessary. But it must be focussed on the task, and firmly controlled.

The Chair must seek to channel conflict: not suppress

it. Never abdicate or take sides, but remain the impartial arbitrator.

Groupthink

Ideas can gain credence within the group simply because a majority of Participants – or the most powerful – support them. Further discussion actually increases the uniformity of opinion. Dissent is stifled.

This has been called the Risky Shift Effect. Agreement is reached at the cost of common sense. The group takes a dangerous decision in the conviction that, if nobody disagrees, it must be the right one. The results can be disastrous. It is usually a committee – in the name of a nation – that declares war.

Symptoms of Groupthink include:

- self-censorship;

- collective rationalization as a source of comfort;

- self-appointed Thoughtguards to suppress dissent on sight;

- pressure on 'deviance' from the norm: overt or covert;

- self-righteousness: taking the moral high ground;

- overweening optimism: a dangerous sense of unassailability.

To counteract Groupthink:

- **Encourage diverse opinions**

- **Pursue disagreements in an orderly way**

- **Invite outsiders or new group members to 'kick-start' change**

- **Examine the procedures of the group: how often you meet; how long since you changed personnel; whether you act democratically**

4

After the Meeting

No meeting is ever an end in itself: it is always part of a process. Very often it will be part of a cycle: meetings result in actions, which provoke change, which itself must be evaluated, calling for new meetings, and so on.

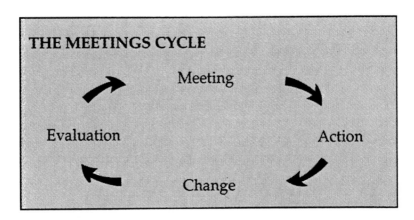

THE MEETINGS CYCLE

Meeting

Evaluation

Action

Change

The Chair: Getting Action

Meetings are judged by their results. The Chair is responsible for ensuring that the actions agreed during the meeting are completed.

Delegate as many actions as possible. This will:

■ relieve you of some of the burden;

■ give ownership of actions to Participants;

■ demonstrate trust;

■ and build the team.

All agreed actions should have a named 'Actioner'. Actioners should feel that they 'own' the action: they should understand why they are doing it and have the authority – and resources – to carry it through. The Chair must ensure that nobody takes on an unrealistic amount of work.

Schedule actions to happen as soon as possible. Prompt action is more likely to be taken by Participants fired with enthusiasm by the meeting they have just left.

All actions should be agreed in the knowledge of:

■ the meeting's and individual's authority to act;

■ the implications for other staff, departments, or organizations;

■ the probable costs;

■ the resources available.

Back up all decisions and actions in writing.

A summary action sheet distributed with – or before – the full minutes can be useful. Others affected by the action may need to be contacted by memo or electronic mail.

You will want to follow up actions at an appropriate time. Don't let follow-up disappear amid all the other fires you have to fight; but take care not to pester, particularly if Participants have volunteered.

Don't simply reschedule uncompleted actions. Discuss the reasons for failure: is the delegated person over-loaded? Perhaps the action was unrealistic or circum-stances suddenly changed.

The Chair has one other main responsibility: overseeing the production of the minutes. This may be a delicate task. You may be tempted to amend the Administrator's first draft: perhaps for diplomatic reasons; sometimes, more sinisterly, for political ones. Minutes which are 'economical with the truth' are unprofessional and unethical. More often the problem falls into a grey area where sensibilities must be tactfully respected while accuracy is maintained.

The Administrator: Writing the Minutes

Lengthy minutes will not be read. Their very name suggests something brief: a summary of events. Minutes are not a word-by-word description of all that is said in a meeting. The term 'verbatim minutes' is a contradiction in terms. A record of every word spoken is a transcript, like Hansard. Minutes are a record of facts, decisions, and agreed actions. Your aim must be to keep the minutes as brief as possible.

Make sure that you are clear from the outset what is required. Check with the Chair on matters of layout and style.

Write up the minutes as soon as possible after the meeting: within 24 hours if you can. They should follow the agenda exactly: with identical numbers and item headings. They might include:

- The name of the meeting
- The venue date and time
- The names of Chair, Administrator, and Participants
- Apologies for absence
  Minutes agreed and signed
- Matters arising
- Summaries of each item
- Summaries of submitted reports
- Motions and amendments

- Proposer's and Seconder's names for each motion or amendment

- Voting numbers

- Decisions reached

- Actions agreed: with names and deadlines

- Venue, date, and time of next meeting

- Date of completion and at least one signature: usually the Chair's. The Administrator's signature is a welcome addition.

Lay out the minutes as attractively as possible. Allow a wide left margin and plenty of space between items. Highlight actions to be taken: perhaps using bold type, underlining, by placing them in a column on the right hand side, or by listing them on a separate sheet.

Constructing a Minute

Background

You must put the item in context for readers who were not at the meeting. The item title may do the job: otherwise, indicate briefly how the matter arose.

Discussion

How much to include? There is no need to attribute statements to particular individuals unless they ask you to do so. You should take care to include references to:

- Recent events

- Dates and place names

- Names of people met or interviewed
- Sums of money
- Legal necessities
- Agreements or contracts
- Policies
- Documentation (reports, correspondence)
- Names of departments or other organizations

Decision

A summary of what has been agreed. There is no need to add lengthy reasons or justification for the decision.

Action

What is to be done: by whom; when; and where. Actions to be highlighted.

Yours will be the definitive record of the meeting. The minutes must satisfy everybody who attended: and this may require a certain amount of tact. Concentrate on facts, decisions and actions, and you will be less likely to go wrong.

Allow yourself time to check the minutes before presenting them to the Chair and distributing them. Check paragraphs, sentence length, unnecessary dialogue, passive verbs and the use of tense.

Paragraphs

Each major contribution to the item will have a separate paragraph. Use sub-paragraphs for substantial amounts of important detail, or lists of points.

As a rough guideline, try not to extend any block of text to more than four lines.

Sentence length

No sentence should be longer than 25 words.

A sentence will probably be too long if it contains too many ideas. Begin by identifying its main idea. Remove everything else: other ideas can be expressed in their own sentences or, if they are less important, can be consigned to oblivion.

Remember: the more important the idea, the more briefly it should be expressed.

Unnecessary dialogue

Avoid the '*He said, she said*' syndrome!

Weed out verbs like: reported, discussed, explained, proposed, expressed concern, suggested, confirmed, requested, asked, introduced, and so on.

Mr Brown reported that he had spoken to the importers on Thursday . . .
Brian and Mary discussed the downturn in sales figures . . .
Geraldine suggested that the options seemed clear. Derek disagreed . . .
Sola expressed concern to Fiona that her team was underperforming. Fiona told Sola . . .

Have you inadvertently slipped into recording what was said – rather than facts or thoughts? What can you remove? What could you put differently or more briefly?

> *Mr Brown spoke to the importers on Thursday ...*
> *Sales figures fell ...*
> *The options for action became clear.*
> *Fiona's team is not underperforming.*

Passive verbs

The curse of minutes everywhere! Of course minutes must be unbiased, but this does not mean that every verb should be passive:

> *Many points of view were expressed...*
> *It was agreed that...*
> *It was thought necessary to...*
> *The resolution however was not passed...*
> *The plans were considered at considerable length...*

Passive verbs describe actions which the subject of the sentence suffers or undergoes. They always consist of a part of the verb To be and a past participle. Many wordprocessing packages now include a 'grammar check' which will identify passive verbs for you.

Wherever possible, substitute active verbs which cut down the length of sentences and accurately allocate responsibility:

> *Everybody expressed their point of view...*
> *The committee agreed that...*
> *We must...*
> *The resolution failed.*
> *The meeting considered the plans at length...*

Tense

Another bone of contention. *'Minutes should be written throughout in the past tense'*, say some authorities. Why?

Certainly statements of what took place during the meeting are best expressed in the past tense:

> *Tom presented a report on current car fleet usage.*

Don't feel, however, that you must rigorously avoid the use of the present tense. The result will be unnatural, cumbersome and almost unreadable:

> *Tom presented a report on current car fleet usage. He revealed that some sales staff had been claiming for unreasonably high mileage figures. After considerable discussion, it was agreed that Tom would continue to monitor expense forms and would report back to the team at the next meeting.*

The minutes, after all, are dated: there is no reason why statements of current information should not be put in the present tense:

> *Some sales staff are still claiming for unreasonably high mileages.*

Use the future for actions to be taken:

> *Tom will continue to monitor expense forms and report back at the next meeting.*

The resulting minute is still accurate: it is now also much easier to read.

Of course minutes need not be written always in full sentences. Provided that meaning is not sacrificed, abbreviated notes can be just as effective:

Tom reported on current car fleet usage. Some sales staff still making unreasonable mileage claims. ACTION: Tom to continue to monitor expense forms, and to report back at next team meeting.

Ambiguous wording

Points made clearly in the meeting may become dangerously ambiguous when condensed into a minute. Watch for:

Vagueness

Most departments are still failing to supply figures . . . (Which departments exactly?)
Several managers have commented adversely on the new system . . . (Who are they?)
Some of the machines are still failing regularly. (How many?)
Staff elsewhere have been notably successful . . . (Where?)
Problems recently/in the near future/at some point . . . (When?)

Euphemism

Delays in delivery are causing some concern.
(How much concern? Is the matter urgent?)
Management is not entirely happy with the new arrangement. (Are they a bit happy? Or actually angry?)

Ambiguous word order

Jeff reported on redirecting sewage to the Works Committee.

After releasing toxic gases into the atmosphere, Bernard reported that his equipment was now in good repair.

Participating After the Meeting

Do you feel that you 'own' the action you have agreed to take? Do you understand why you are doing the job? Are you empowered to do it? You must have the necessary:

- Authority

- Instructions

- Resources

- Budget

- Staff

- Information

- **Show willing**
  If you don't, you may get picked on!

- **Don't take on too much**
  You may fail and praise may turn to mockery.

- **Act promptly**
  Don't delay. You may forget vital information. Circumstances may change sooner than you think and make the job even more complicated.

- **Report back as agreed:**
  Either directly to the Chair or at the next meeting.

- **Liaise**
  Your actions may well link to those of others who

were at the meeting and will probably form the basis for future agenda items.

Finally: do you feel that your contribution is being recognized and appreciated? If not: proclaim your success!

Different Meetings and How to Run Them

Team Meetings

Teams must meet frequently. The danger for any regular meeting is that it can collapse into a routine: soon it comes to be regarded more with dread than interest.

The solution might be to change the way the meetings are run. A team leader who is willing to delegate functions to other team members will lead meetings that are more active, more involving and more successful.

Remember: the aim of any regular meeting must be to keep it as short as possible. How to do it:

- The team leader constructs the agenda informally prior to the meeting. Anyone who wants to contribute sends a note or adds it to the list. E-mail is particularly valuable for this.

- The agenda is finalized at the start of the meeting. Each Participant must justify the inclusion of their item on the agenda. The meeting decides whether it is worthy of discussion: perhaps another team member can solve the problem outside the meeting: a brief conversation, a memo, a report put in the internal post.

- All items decided on for the agenda are given timings. The whole meeting has a maximum length – decided upon by the team leader – which it must not exceed. The aim is not to fill the allotted time, but to complete the meeting as quickly as possible.

- The agenda is now complete. Nothing else is allowed until the next meeting.

- Each item is 'owned' by the Participant who submitted it. They become the Chair for that item. As discussion progresses, they must ask:
  - is the task or problem clearly understood?
  - is expertise identified?
  - is knowledge shared?
  - are they creating a cooperative climate in the group?
  - is everyone being heard?
  - can a decision be reached by consensus without a vote)?
  - is the Chair's role reduced to a minimum?

- The Chair for each item becomes the minute-taker for the next item, recording the minutes on a flip chart for all to see.

- Timings are strictly adhered to and are the responsibility of the team as a whole.

- At the end of the meeting, decisions and actions are summarized by the team leader who then invites any initial suggestions for the next meeting.

The result of this procedure is increased ownership of the meeting by the whole team. A climate of openness allows all views to be expressed with equal authority; solutions are arrived at by consensus rather than imposed. In one company where it was introduced, the time spent in team meetings was cut by a third.

Problem Solving

Meetings solve problems all the time. Sometimes, though, a meeting will be called to address a single, specific problem.

The process of solving a problem can be broken down into four separate activities:

- analysis: studying, defining and categorizing the problem

- imagination: generating optional solutions

- criticism: evaluating the options and discarding some

- judgement: deciding which option to pursue

1.   Identify the problem

Make it public: the group must 'own' the problem collectively.

Define it positively. Not *'we are in danger of losing our biggest customer'*; but *'how do we retain our most valued client?'*

2.   Analyse it

Break the problem down into categories and put them in order. Distinguish between hard facts and people's opinions.

3.   Set an objective

Are you going to solve the whole problem at this meeting – or only a part of it? Consider:

- the ideal solution

- a realistic solution

- a fallback position

Gain agreement on the objective. Remind the meeting of the agreed objective when the going gets tough.

4. Consider various solutions

Play with the problem: turn it around, upside down, inside out. Look at different aspects. Take care not to evaluate solutions. When criticism of a solution begins to appear, the Chair must move on to other suggestions.

5. Evaluate solutions

Don't rush to conclusions. Test groups who were asked to find a second solution after having 'solved' the problem always came up with something better. Evaluate each solution in terms of impact, cost, resources, and simplicity. You might want to make lists of advantages and disadvantages of each solution on a flip chart.

6. Choose a solution

Which has the most or best advantages, and least disadvantages? What are the benefits of this solution?

7. Decide how to implement it

Who owns it? Perhaps various parts of the solution will be owned by different people. Are they happy to take ownership? Are they competent to do the job? Have they the resources?

Set actions with names and deadlines.

8. Set date for next meeting

To consider the effectiveness of the solution.

Brainstorming Sessions

Unlike problem solving, which works towards a single solution, brainstorming aims to generate as many ideas as possible without evaluating or deciding on any.

It was developed by Alex Osborn in the 1950s and promoted by, among others, Edward de Bono as a forum for Lateral Thinking.

Use brainstorming sessions:

- in the search for an innovative solution;

- at the beginning of a meeting, to break the ice;

- to strengthen a team.

Follow these rules for a successful brainstorming session:

- Keep it short – 30 minutes is ideal – with a strict time limit.

- Not too many participants: 6 – 12 is about right.

- Include as wide a range of people as possible. Do bear in mind that the presence of senior management can be inhibiting.

- Seats are best best in a semi-circle with no tables. Chair sitting anywhere; Administrator standing at a flip chart.

- The Chair must:
    - stop everyone talking at once;
    - make sure quieter participants contribute;
    - prevent evaluation of ideas;
    - redefine problems at various points in meeting;
    - check that the Administrator has every idea;
    - be ready with ideas when the flow stops;
    - ask for a review of ideas when the flow dries up;
    - bring the session to a close.

- The Administrator must:
    - note down every idea contributed;
    - condense them for inclusion on the list;
    - check with Participants on meaning;
    - demand a pause if they can't keep up;
    - never refuse to list an idea, even if they feel it repeats an earlier one;
    - not contribute any ideas of their own.

- No analysis of the problem is allowed.

- No evaluation of ideas is allowed: on the basis of relevance, quality of idea, practicality, common sense or anything else.

An experienced group can generate up to 200 ideas in thirty minutes. These are analysed, later, in an evaluation session:

- List the obviously useful ideas.

- Dismiss ideas which have already been tried and failed.

- Note ideas which can be tried easily, immediately – and cheaply.

- Note promising ideas.

- List ideas needing further thought or research.

- Extract useful aspects from silly ideas. These may produce new ideas.

The result of a brainstorming session should be new lists of ideas for immediate trial and ideas for further exploration.

Consultative Meetings

Whenever a consultant or expert meets with a client to present a proposal, however uncommercial the situation, something is being 'sold'. Consequently, the meeting will include a good deal of presentation.

The meeting will fail completely if the client's requirements are not adequately defined beforehand. Part of the consultant's job will very often be to help the client clarify just what they do want.

Preparation is essential. Get to know the client's field of operations, their history, their style, their current situation (successful? losing market share?). Ask the basic questions:

- why do they want help?

- who has the authority, the budget, and the willingness to implement the solution we propose? Are we talking to them?

- what exactly do they want? What can they afford?

- when do they want it?

- where will it be implemented? In one department, or throughout the organization?

- how do they envisage us contributing? Once or over a period of time? As consultants, trainers, auditers, publishers, engineers?

A pre-meeting meeting is vital, to define the problem and agree the client's requirements as clearly as possible. This will probably be confirmed in a document sent to the client before the meeting.

As for the meeting itself:

1.   Create rapport with the client

Show an understanding of their situation: their industry, their corporate culture. Show how you fit in: your credentials, your expertise, other clients you've worked for.

2.   Identify the client's need

Define the problem – as agreed in the pre-meeting meeting, and in your written proposal. Demonstrate how willing and eager you are to take on the burden.

3.   Present your solution

In summary, broken down into its major parts. Briefly explain why this is the right solution for this situation.

4.   Explain the proposal in detail

Go through the proposal stage by stage, emphasizing end-results for the client rather than the details of how you will achieve them.

Remember: you are selling peace of mind.

5.   Anticipate any objections you know the client has

Answer them before they are raised. But be careful not to create objections that the client may not have thought of for themselves! You will sow the seeds of doubt.

6.   Restate the proposal

Summarize. Invite a discussion.

7.   Keep discussion separate from your presentation

You will be in a much stronger position to answer the client's questions.

8.   What will happen at the end of the meeting?

Can the client make a decision on the spot? Will your message now have to be sold by them to somebody else? Who will contact whom?

What is the next stage in the process?

Mealtime Meetings

Business lunches, and now breakfast meetings, are increasingly popular: on the whole, however, they are of limited value. The meeting must of necessity be informal: it will be difficult to take minutes while negotiating coq au vin. There will probably be no written agenda; the objective of the meeting may be unclear. The professional and social aspects of meeting are dangerously mixed. Hidden agendas are probably hard at work.

- Decide on your own private agenda. Are you going to meet − or eat?

- If the meeting is worth attending, you must be prepared not to eat anything. Talking with your mouth full could prove disastrous.

- Avoid alcohol.

- Taking notes will be difficult. Arm yourself with a narrow pad which can slip easily between plates and glasses.

Electronic Meetings

These can be held either over the telephone or via a video link and are designed to cut costs; but they obviously rely on all the Participants being in place, on time.

■ Allow pauses between speakers

A single word overlapping another speaker will cause considerable delay while the last remark is repeated. A teleconference has its own, peculiar rhythm which is easily picked up with a little practice.

■ Use names frequently

Announce yourself by name: particularly if you haven't spoken for some time. Announce whom you are addressing, and who you would like to speak next.

■ Choose your words with care

The fact that people are not physically together places great weight on the words used. There is a lot of opportunity for misunderstanding and much may need to be laboriously explained in the absence of a visual component.

■ **Avoid hidden agendas**

Teleconferences without video are vulnerable to conspiracies: notes passed silently between Participants in one room, gestures and facial expressions mocking the ignorance of those at the other end of the line. Order must be maintained. On the other hand, it can sometimes be easier to be brutally frank when the other person is five hundred miles away.

■ **On video, ensure that everybody is visible**

Hidden voices and disembodied hands swimming into shot are distracting.

Multicultural Meetings

Here are three managers describing meetings with their colleagues. In each case the manager and the colleagues are of different nationalities. Can you decide in each case which nationality is describing which?

CASE STUDY ONE

I put a lot of time into studying the reports before the meeting. It is evident that my colleagues at the meeting are examining the papers for the first time. It wastes all our time. But it doesn't stop them giving their opinions.

> ## CASE STUDY TWO
>
> My staff meetings are very annoying. It is very hard to get them to stick to the agenda. And they insist on discussing every point until everyone has had their say.

> ## CASE STUDY THREE
>
> You have the impression that they don't realize that they're at a meeting. They don't pay attention or they interrupt or they get up and make a phone call.

(Answers at the end of this chapter.)

These examples are taken from John Mole's excellent book, *Mind Your Manners*, which examines different cultures in the European Community and is invaluable for anybody working across cultural boundaries. Many of the ideas in this section are his.

Different cultures exist within one country, of course: sensitivity to a person's background is a prerequisite of modern business practice. In some cases, cultural differences will be overlaid by a homogeneous corporate culture. John Mole identifies two areas which particularly determine the way people interact at work:

■ Beliefs about the organization

How is the company structured? How does it plan? How is information disseminated? How are results measured?

■ Beliefs about leadership

Who has power? How do they justify their authority? Who takes decisions?

Meetings between organizations with noticeably different cultures have their own problems.

Behaviour in meetings will also be determined by other factors:

■ Individual background

Consider the values each individual brings with them into the room: family values, religious or ethical values, considerations of education, etiquette, respect for others, the way work is carried out.

■ National or ethnic background

Behind each person stands the history of their country, their ethnic group or people. It is impossible to ignore the wider tensions (or friendships) which may exist between national or ethnic groups, or the history which may have brought people together.

Each meeting should aim to create common ground between those who attend it. The objectives of the meeting should be realistic and work-oriented: but it is also a chance for people to increase their understanding of each other. The best way to minimize culture clash is to make sure that the purpose of the meeting is made crystal clear, and that procedures within the meeting accommodate everybody's expectations.

Language

The meeting will probably be held in one language. Anybody not fluent in that language will feel seriously disadvantaged. The choice of language for the meeting can itself be a serious cultural or even political matter. Arrange for papers to be translated if necessary. You may decide that speakers can speak in any language comprehensible to all, or that they should bring personal translators with them.

Preparation

Different business cultures create different expectations of meetings. For some, the most important work is conducted outside the meeting: at dinner the night before, or in the coffee break. Your procedures may need to allow for this, by scheduling social events before or after the meeting.

Distribute papers well in advance with specific

requests for comments. This will give you some idea of the nature of Participants' preparation.

During the meeting

Don't be alarmed if people seem to behave oddly. What may seem unacceptably rude to you – leaving the meeting without warning to make a phone call, disregarding formal procedure, writing a letter while others are speaking – may be normal behaviour in another culture.

Agree the agenda before and at the start of the meeting. Pay special attention to the purpose of individual items, who will speak to them, and what decisions are expected from each. Announce how you expect people to contribute.

After the meeting

Getting agreement on decisions or actions is notoriously problematic in cross-cultural meetings. Are people agreeing to act, or being polite? What is being agreed to? Does each side fully intend to act as they say they will? Sometimes confusion exists between passive consensus, which is agreement to a course of action, and active consensus, where people are fully committed to carrying it out.

You must make sure that decisions are specific and understood. In a matter as crucial as a contract, you may even want to take legal advice. Make sure that actions are agreed by named individuals, and that you have clear procedures for follow-up.

In any meeting between cultures, the overwhelming danger is in reinforcing stereotypes. As John Mole says:

'Whether or not they exist in reality, stereotypes certainly exist in the perception of outsiders. And it is in perceptions of behaviour that misunderstandings occur. Avoiding them will make collaboration not necessarily more harmonious but at least more productive.'

Answers:

■ Case Study One: A Dutch engineer referring to British colleagues.

■ Case Study Two: The French manager of an Italian company.

■ Case Study Three: The English director of a Franco-British company.

Appendix A: Agendas and Minutes

Right Now Couriers

Business Review Meeting: Thursday 6 January, 6pm – 7.30pm.

To attend: Sam Butcher – Chair
Richard Rogerson
Brian Josephs
Dierdre Smith
Steve Robbins
Sue Newcombe – Administrator

1.   New Business

Steve to report on;
  (a) Mailings
  (b) Telephone calls
  (c) Presentations   [**15 mins.**]

Discussion to agree new business actions and marketing materials. Please bring your ideas.   [**15 mins.**]

2.   Systems and equipment

Sam to report on current status.   [**10 mins.**]

Discussion to agree actions on the above.   [**10 mins.**]

3.   People

Brian to report on resourcing needs.   [**10 mins.**]

Decision to be taken to implement recommendations.   [**10 mins.**]

4.   Finance

Dierdre to report on funding needed to implement agreed actions.   [**10 mins.**]

Decide on funding agreed actions.   [**10 mins.**]

7.30   Close

Please bring your diary with you.

Right Now Couriers

Minutes of the Business Review Meeting, Thursday 6 January at 6pm.

Present: Sam Butcher – Chair
              Richard Rogerson
              Brian Josephs
              Dierdre Smith
              Steve Robbins
              Sue Newcombe – Administrator

By	*Item*	*Action*
	1. New business	
6 Feb	Mailings. New business to be limited to Central London. New mailings to design agencies, hardware dealers.	Steve
10 Jan	Telephone marketing: behind schedule. Investigate part-time support.	Brian
31 Mar	Presentations: five booked for January. Target of five per month.	Steve

By	*Item*	*Action*
	2. Systems and equipment	
31 Jan	Replace docket system with network.	Sam
20 Jan	Replace aerial in W12.	Richard
15 Feb	New vans. Write finance implications paper.	Dierdre
	3. People	
1 Feb	Recruit new van driver.	Sam
1 Feb	Draw up loyalty bonus scheme.	Brian
9 Feb	International specialist. Discuss at next meeting.	All
	4. Finance	
14 Jan	Research NI implications of recruitment plan.	Steve

By	*Item*	*Action*
	Secure finance for new systems.	Dierdre
Feb		

5.   Date of next meeting

9 February, 6pm at Right now. Write agenda. Sam
1 Feb

Appendix B: Auditing Meetings

Very few organizations audit meetings. Yet it is probably an area where major cost benefits will result from systematic evaluation.

Avoid informal post-mortems which tend to degenerate into personal attacks. Evaluation must be objective and conducted by the whole group. It must be conducted in a separate forum from the meetings themselves. Above all, the group as a whole must decide that it wants to improve and everybody must accept responsibility for change.

The most obvious basis for a meetings audit is a questionnaire, to be filled in anonymously and privately by all participants directly after each meeting.

Each question is marked using a sliding scale:

(*Not at all*) 1   2   3   4   5   6 (*Completely*)

Use an even number of points to avoid the drift towards an uncommitted middling score.

- Was the meeting necessary?

- Was the objective of the meeting clear?

- Did it meet its objective?

- Was it the right length?

- Was it held at a convenient time?

- Did it start and finish on time?

- Was the venue convenient?

- Were the venue facilities adequate?

- Did you receive the agenda in good time?

- Was the agenda adequately detailed?

- Did the meeting follow the agenda?

- Were all the right people present?

- Were you given sufficient notice?

- Were you sent all the information you needed?

- Were you sent all the papers you needed?

- Was timekeeping satisfactory?

- Did the Chair exercise appropriate control?

- Were the meeting notes taken well?

- Was the decision-making procedure satisfactory?

- Were the actions resulting from the meeting clear?

- Were the minutes distributed promptly?

At the meeting audit:

- Review what worked well. Praise accordingly.

- Identify areas for improvement.

- Resolve: what to do more; what to do less; what to do differently. Allocate areas of responsibility.

- Ensure that the changes agreed are reviewed after the next meeting.

Meeting

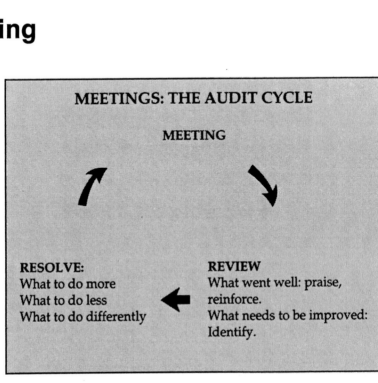

MEETINGS: THE AUDIT CYCLE

MEETING

RESOLVE:
What to do more
What to do less
What to do differently

REVIEW
What went well: praise, reinforce.
What needs to be improved: Identify.

You can conduct a meetings audit much more effectively using an external auditor. They will be able to observe more dispassionately, identifying what is working well and what needs to change. They are also able to communicate with the group as a whole, challenging ingrained habit and giving advice on how to improve.

The Industrial Society offers a wide range of training and consultancy in every aspect of meetings. It runs training courses both publicly and in-house, and can act as an independent auditor of meetings in your organization. For further details please contact:

The Industrial Society
48 Bryanston Square
London W1H 7LN

Telephone: 071 262 2401

Bibliography

Mole, John, *Mind Your Manners*, London: Nicholas Brealey Publishing, 1991
John Mole's best-selling book offers shrewd and perceptive advice on how to operate in European countries separated by much more than just language. A Finanical Times Business Book of the Year in 1991.

de Bono, Edward, *Lateral Thinking for Management*, London: Penguin, 1982

Brown, Paul, and Hackett, Fiona, *Managing Meetings*, London: Fontana, 1990

Gratus, Jack, *Give and Take*, London: BBC, 1990

Hodgson, Philip and Jane, *Effective Meetings*, London: Century Press, 1992

Honey, P, *Improve Your People Skills*, London: Institute of Personnel Management, 1988

Maude, Barry, *Managing Meetings* London: Business Books, 1975

Minto, Barbara, *The Pyramid Principle*, London: Pitman, 1987

Mole, John, *Mind Your Manners*, London: The Industrial Society, 1990

Mort, Simon, *The Minutes*, Aldershot: Gower, 1991

Sharman, David, *The Perfect Meeting*, London: Century Business, 1993

Ward, Sue, *A-Z of Meetings: How they work and how to run them*, London: Pluto Press, 1985